jane and louise wilson

MINIGRAPHS is a series of publications developed by ellipsis and Film and Video Umbrella devoted to contemporary artists from Britain who work primarily in the area of film and video. The series builds on a previous partnership in which ellipsis, as publishers, and Film and Video Umbrella, as project producers, joined forces to release a number of innovative digital art works, packaged as a CD-ROM with an accompanying book, on the label ●●● electric art. These new publications, while linking with 'Film and Video Artists on Tour', a programme of public presentations by each of the featured artists, are nevertheless designed to stand on their own, offering a concise and illuminating overview of the artists' influences and preoccupations and highlighting the growing interest in film and video within contemporary visual art.

We would like to thank the National Lottery through the Arts Council of England and London Film and Video Development Agency for their support of this initiative.

Tom Neville, ●●●ellipsis
Steven Bode, Film and Video Umbrella

jane and louise wilson

with essays by jeremy millar and claire doherty

●●●ellipsis

First published 2000 by

●●● ellipsis

2 Rufus Street

London N1 6PE

EMAIL ...@ellipsis.co.uk

www.ellipsis.com

A collaboration with Film and Video Umbrella, published to accompany the Film and Video Umbrella touring project 'Film and Video Artists on Tour'

This publication was supported by the National Lottery through the Arts Council of England

film and video umbrella

ISBN 1 84166 027 2

Design by Claudia Schenk

Printed and bound in Spain by Gráficas Varona

●●● ellipsis is a trademark of Ellipsis London Limited

British Library Cataloguing in Publication Data: a CIP record for this publication is available from the British Library

For a copy of the Ellipsis catalogue or information on special quantity orders of Ellipsis books please contact sales on 020 7739 3157 or sales@ellipsis.co.uk

contents

the story so far

jeremy millar

So, where were we? Where did we get to? It's sometimes difficult to keep track, with so much happening all around, to keep track of where I've had to go, or whom I've spoken to. And then what I've told you. Sometimes I think it would be better if there were two of me (that would be useful) just to keep check. Maybe I should just carry on and see where we end up, see where we've got. I knew that this wouldn't be easy when they first asked me about it, so many uncertainties, so many stories, so many clues. So many things to think about, to follow up, so many things to consider. And then you can never really believe what you hear. Or what you read.

I received a large envelope which contained a ream of photocopies, a videotape, other bits and pieces. I started looking through the photo-copied material, much of which I recognised, stapling sections together, and soon realised that there were two copies of everything, which made me a little uneasy. Was one set for someone else? Perhaps I'm not the only one. I checked to see whether there were any discrepancies between the copies, different parts marked, but at that time it was diffi-cult to tell them apart. I put one copy back in the envelope, the other in a card folder I'd prepared earlier. On the front I had already written: 'Something is uncanny – that is how it begins. But at the same time one must search for that "remoter" something which is already close at hand.' The quotation is from Bloch, from 'A Philosophical View of the Detective Novel', and I put it there just to remind me.

•••

It took a while before access to the Executive Buildings was granted. They were empty at this time in any case, the country being run, as it always is, under fluorescent tubes in other places. Everything seemed somewhat familiar, from television actually, and so it was interesting the number of televisions here as well. The screens were magnet-grey at the time but we were told that when the Executive Chamber was in use, then that would be shown upon the screens. They were often on shelves or brackets, high up on a wall, like curved security mirrors, offering a strange reflection upon security itself. And there were mirrors too, of course, throughout the building, acting as both corridors and dead-ends, and often reflecting back the television screens, or ornate doors which themselves screened from view other television screens. Or tape machines, hearing devices.

Telephones too, everywhere, a cream one near the chair of the door-keeper, who will also open the door at the knocking of Black Rod; a

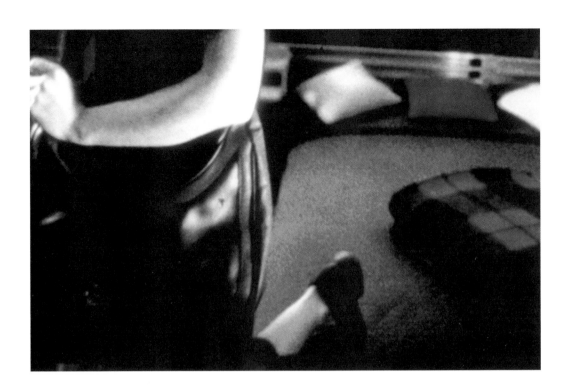

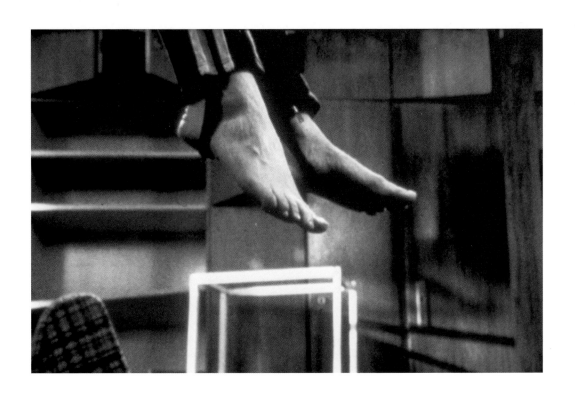

brown one beyond sliding doors for the Peers. A row of cubicles also for the press, twelve of them, one for each newspaper. A small piece of paper, the size of an identity card, is slotted into a brass frame on the outside of each door, although I could only make out one: 'Daily Mail E.I.C.Y. 23073'. To which other exchanges do these lines connect? Behind which other doors are these conversations heard?

We walked back along the corridors, the deep red carpets marked by strange areas of light and dark along their patterned lengths, perhaps the ephemeral forms left by now-absent human flows. Other flows move elsewhere, hot air from the chambers rising through holes in the ceiling and through to the towers, little more than gothic chimneys. A periscope surveys the chambers, its strange perspective curving the space, liquefying it, perhaps, bringing opposite sides together. Below ground this plumbing continues, clad pipes cladding the corridors, like some stretched padded cell. Noises are heard though they seem to come from far away. We follow them, never finding them, though they find us, follow us round, until we begin to recognise these identical places once more. Much later, I find amongst my notes:

'A small picture presented the interior of an immensely long and rectangular vault or tunnel, with low walls, smooth white, and without interruption or device. Certain accessory points of the design served well to convey that this excavation lay at an exceeding depth below the surface of the earth. No outlet was observed in any portion of its vast extent, and no torch or other artificial source of light was discernible; yet a flood of intense rays rolled throughout and bathed the whole in a ghastly and inappropriate splendour.'

It is in my handwriting, although I didn't write it.

●●●

'I still saw the room where I was but I was completely indifferent to it. Space seemed to stretch out, to grow in infinity; but at the same time it was emptied of its content … I felt absolutely alone and abandoned, overwhelmed and consigned to infinite space, which, despite its ephemeral nature, rose up menacingly before me. It was before me in an immediate way, the complement of my own emptiness and my mental breakdown … I felt a swirling in front of me, or, more precisely, I felt myself whirling in a narrow limited space. This swirling was in motion and was immobile at the same time. Simultaneously, time and the former tangible space of which I spoke above, and which was a function of the other space, disappeared.'

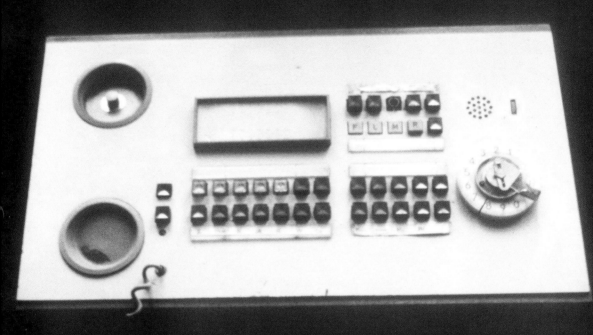

•••

He was quite pale, the man, with skin like wax, lit dully from within. We had seen him a number of times as he kept walking past where we were, although he seemed to do this without intention, as his repeated surprise was visible (I couldn't tell you where we were). Every now and then, the light above us shivered. He sat nearby and began talking. Although quiet, his voice was strong. It was clear, even if it wasn't clear what he was saying.

Our presence was unnecessary as he would have talked regardless; he didn't look at us as he spoke, although I'm not sure he would have seen us even if he had. His head rocked slightly, firmly, marking out an internal rhythm; his eyes looked up and out towards the buildings as their failing outlines dissolved into the surrounding dark. Perhaps they offered a guide, more likely a warning. He spoke of gaol, of imprisonment, although I wasn't sure that he was talking of himself; even when he used the first person, he wasn't the first person who came to mind. Lines were repeated, whole sections repeated, over and over, as though trying to solidify them, not to memorise them, but to make them less fluid in fact, to give them substance, a shape of their own, perhaps so that they can be recognised separate from him (or that he could be recognised as separate from them).

He began to slide from our attention and we continued our conversation … about film, and architecture, about narrative and its repetitions (about *Last Year at Marienbad*). About spaces real and imaginary, about real spaces which seem to be in a place other than their location. It is only weeks later that I listen to the tape, when it is too late, when the other two have gone. It is only weeks later that I find our voices muffled under the voice of another:

'Creeping along the sides of the wall, you perceived a staircase; and upon it, groping his way upwards, was Piranesi himself: follow the stairs a little further, and you perceive it come to a sudden abrupt termination, without any balustrade, and allowing no step onwards to him who had reached the extremity, except into the depths below. Whatever is to become of poor Piranesi, you suppose, at least, that his labours must in some way terminate here. But raise your eyes, and behold a second flight of stairs still higher: on which again Piranesi is perceived, by this time standing on the very brink of the abyss. Again elevate your eye, and a still more aerial flight of stairs is beheld and again is poor Piranesi busy on his aspiring labours: and so on, until the unfinished stairs and Piranesi are lost in the upper gloom of the hall.

'Oh, how will he make his way, the poor Piranesi, between these close-pressing beams and fragile scaffolds that bend and creak? How will he advance across these unstable paths that are joined to each other by narrow and shaky joists? … across this mass of ill-laid stones that overhang and beneath these low and perilous vaults …? One would follow with unease the subtle path of the lightest lizard!

'Piranesi climbs nevertheless, and, even though the mind can hardly imagine it, Piranesi arrives. – He arrives, alas, at the foot of a building similar to the first, access to which presents the same difficulties, menacing him with the same perils, demanding the same effort, in yet greater proportion, magnified by his tiredness, exhaustion, and also his old age … Nevertheless, Piranesi climbs again; he must climb and climb and arrive. – And he arrives.

'He arrives overburdened, decrepit, broken, feeble as a shadow; he has arrived at the bottom level of a building similar to the first buildings …'

•••

'… it appeared to me that pure calculation means fairly little and has none of the importance many gamblers attach to it. They sit over bits of paper ruled into columns, note down the coups, count up, compute probabilities, do sums, finally put down their stakes and – lose exactly the same as we poor mortals playing without calculation. But on the other hand I drew one conclusion, which I think is correct: in a series of pure chances there really does exist, if not a system, at any rate a sort of sequence – which is of course very odd.'

•••

'The gambler. Time squirts out of his every pore.'

I couldn't tell you how long we've been here, waiting. There's little else to do, despite everything that's happening. Even when we're actually doing something, even when we don't realise it, we're actually just waiting. Killing time, I guess, although it's actually more of a suicide pact, between time and ourselves, although we can never be

quite sure that it will actually keep its side of the bargain.

We seem to be caught between different experiences of time, different speeds. The desert, this immense landscape which surrounds us, appears both outside of time and yet so obviously subject to it. Here in the city, electricity stretches time, accelerates it, many days seeming like one, while one can last many days. They repeat, and we are caught in that repetition, but they are never quite the same. Things come round again.

I move round the building, through the building, and though I'm not necessarily looking for a way out, there isn't one immediately obvious in any case. The spaces seem huge, opening endlessly in all directions like some architectural Big Bang. And then they contract, banks of mirrors reflected in other mirrors and everything suddenly becomes more dense, images of people caught within the lattices of crystalline space. I have given up trying to look for the other two, though they must be caught here also. I catch sight of them, yes, perhaps one, perhaps both, yet they fragment further and further, disappearing into the corner of two mirrors, becoming part of the space itself. A figure flows down an escalator, although the sound is of water. Blocks of light slide along the floor, raising parts of its surface, dissolving the rest. I seem to be floating.

Round we come again, round roulette wheels, round the curves of stairs, reflected back in mirrors which curve the space further. Round the starbursts in the carpets, round the explosions beneath our feet. Round chandeliers and round again.

•••

'Have not its incessant vagabondages accustomed the city to proffer a new interpretation of its image everywhere? Does it not transform the passage into a casino, into a gaming house?'

The voice quietens, the tape stops.

•••

In a place called Z—, near N—, we enter an office building. The space is full of dust, slightly aerated inside the open-plan, there are groups of men and women, in clothes the colour of furniture. We can hear the blood moving through our ears. We are met by P—, a large man who appears smaller than he actually is, certainly smaller than he was. His trousers and tie are both grey; his v-neck is blue, perhaps woollen, and bears the marks of cigarettes, as do his fingers, his teeth, his eyes. He goes through the plan, through the open-plan.

From around a half partition the space opens once again, and we see rows of long trestle tables, scaled-up toy insects, scraps of paper covering their backs like scales. Men and women are grooming them, silently, repairing them. Some are wearing face masks. Movements are slowly considered, slow and considered, then quick and sure, a scrap reclaimed and then joined with tape to another, or others.

'We pieced together 180,000 pages in our first 16 months here,' P— says as we walk along one side of the room, careful not to move too closely, too quickly, to the tables. Some of those there look up at us, through us, obliged in some way. 'Some of the files were shredded, but so fast was the collapse that most were simply torn into pieces, maybe eight, or twelve, or more, depending on the folds.' There are no windows; the lights in the ceiling make the room green, as though it had been photographed.

We move towards a door which P— opens. We enter the small hallway on the other side, P— closing the door behind us. He moves back through us, pressing the button for the lift which opens perhaps a few seconds later. He moves to the side, a tired smile, and then his left arm moves slightly, hand open. We go in. The doors close as he places a key in a button near the bottom of the stainless-steel control panel, a button he then pushes. Our bodies tell us they are floating, until they tell us that we've stopped. The doors open and we look out on to the hallway which it seems we have just come from. We follow P— into it, looking at each other, noncommittally, while he unlocks the door. This time he enters first.

The air seems much cooler, although I'm uncertain if this is simply a psychological consequence of the higher ceiling and concrete floor. Bright ice-white lights emphasise the outlines of the shelves, row upon row, which stand like bureaucratic monoliths, some late-historical assemblage, in the hangar space. Black files make these spaces more dense. There is a guard standing to the left, near but not against the wall, although he ignores us. Words, numbers, letters are stencilled upon the wall, above his head and to his left, into the distance, perhaps marking and naming each zone. I look elsewhere. Tracks of yellow lines run down the centre of the image, a painted crease, more shelves are reflected in the other space which this threshold marks. I hand the picture back, noticing my perfect thumbprint on the back of the grey metal racks. She puts it back into a file, like those in the photograph, and takes another out as part of the same movement, holding it out to me. I move to take it but it seems that I can only look this time. It's hard to make out what's happening here; a room of sorts, quite dark, although the light upon the floor is perhaps the most obvious element; some objects, somewhat familiar, although not altogether recognisable. Is that a bicycle wheel? A toilet? (Is this some kind of art joke, a trap perhaps? Am I supposed to realise what is going on here? I try to make that gesture which suggests that I do, that slight nod of acknowledgement that we might make to a vague acquaintance as they pass us at a gathering of sorts.) She stares at me intently, her gaze questioning what it is that I know, and whether there is anything that I might add. Her question becomes its own answer. At this, her hand retracts and the picture becomes smaller and darker. She turns away.

I remain seated, looking around the room. The light seems to be made more of darkness, a smudge across the surface of things. The paint on the ceiling bubbles and blooms, breaking open like a skin disease. In the corner is a kitchen sink set into a cupboard; one of the doors below is open, an empty shelf and a corpse of rags. The walls are covered with two different wallpaper patterns, both the colour of tobacco. One pattern is small, like insects squashed against its surface. The other is slightly lighter, the repetition seemingly more regular (although perhaps it is just easier to fix these larger shapes in my head). I become caught in their repetition, moving from one to the other, hypnotised by the regularity of rhythm, the same, again, and again, the same. My eyes begin to scan along the lines, trying to read their differences, a patch of damp casting internal shadows, or a constellation of oily marks reflected in the pissy afternoon light. I try to find other patterns below or above or within the obvious ones. I become convinced that in here, somewhere, is described the cycle in which I keep finding myself, described, perhaps, no, not described but directed, certain instead that each mark, each barely noticed shape in some way sets out the workings of my own future. That it should be here. I feel haunted.

'That's it exactly,' she answers. 'Ghosts of the future are the only sort worth heeding. Apparitions of things past are a very unpractical sort of demonology, in my opinion, compared with apparitions of things to come.' The sound of trains from the station nearby wakes me, wakes the building, and there in the empty room, my eyes burn with the stench of afternoon.

•••

'The air is still there, the air between the objects in the room. But the objects themselves are not there. Sometimes I have to think about the various objects in order: the bed rail, the pillow, the wall, the window, etc. And each time the thing of which I am thinking goes away. An empty space is added to the others, and then everything is there all the same. Sometimes, also, everything is there all the same. Sometimes, also, everything is empty. The whole sea that the universe is, is emptied too, and I am afraid.'

•••

I began arguing with myself as I walked through the empty rooms, although such interrogations seldom ended satisfactorily. The fear of boredom split like cancer and became boredom then fear; like life, as the poet said. I convinced myself that these rooms weren't empty, although I saw no-one, but were inhabited not only by strange inventories but also by their own sense of themselves. Rooms began to fill with the noise of silent objects. Scattered debris, the things left over, no longer of use, became the ingredients of some perverse new game.

They stare at me. The tape loops turn. I continue.

There was some lighting flex (I thought that might come in handy) and a spoon (maybe), but then some gum, chewed, in a jar. Things were hanging from the ceiling: a pulley holding a bag, and another bag, which I couldn't reach, which had, let's just say it had something in it. Another bag, just like it, sat on the floor, bloody stains on the wall above showing where it had hit and fallen.

The tape loops turn.

A sock full of bricks, a chair tipped up and with only one leg, like a tortured insect. But then shelves protected by plastic. The questions I asked myself, the questions I asked of myself. The questions these rooms asked of me. How many clues had they left for me? How many had I discovered (have I discovered)? Everything became a new possibility. A saucepan. A bottle of lighter fluid (especially the lighter fluid). The pot of glue.

Tape loops turn.

The whole building was infested and began to swarm in front of my eyes. I began to drown in its movements. I sank

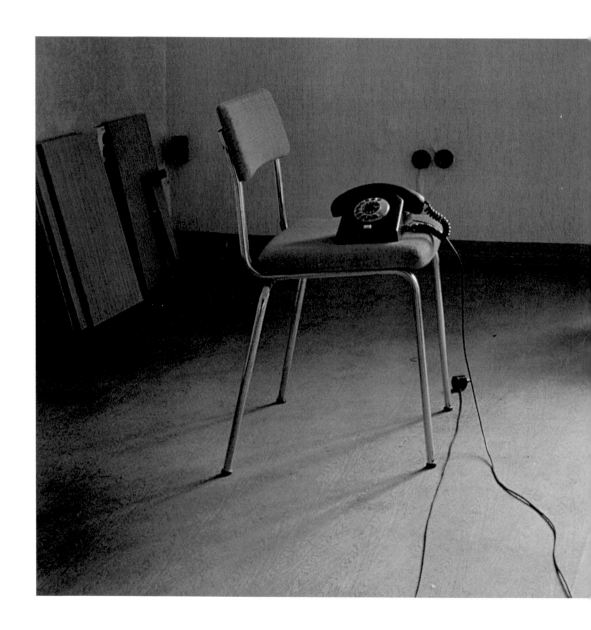

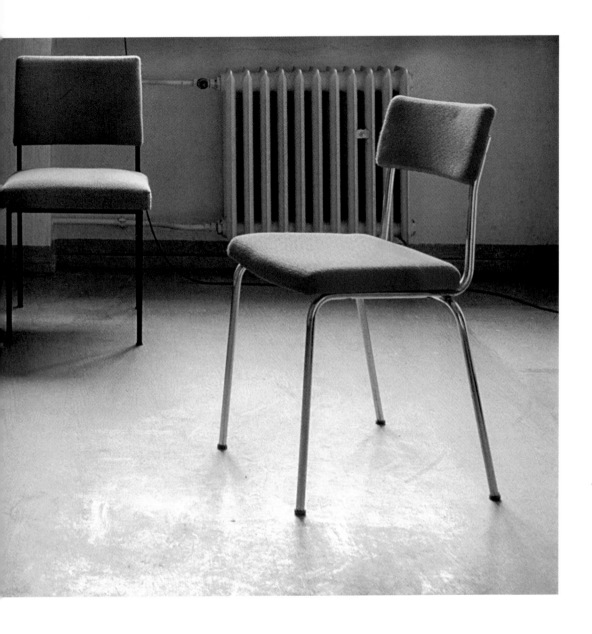

back down stairs and there, now, then, was a letter, a newspaper, a plug even, where there was none before (I'm sure none before). The phone hanging also, as though someone was attempting to say something, and then stopped ... Had this just happened? Were these things evidence of a crime or its preparations? What else had been decided? Where was I going to be when it happened?

Loops turn.

And then I realised, it was already happening, to me to begin with, then by me. The walls seemed to breath, swelling with life. I began to absorb its rhythms, the sharp impulses and the slow unfoldings, neuron sparks and blood flows, and continue then. Each object was written in the past tense but opened up on to the possibilities of the future.

Loops.

I began to think, as Pascal had once thought (was only able to now because Pascal had then), that all evil in men comes from one thing and one thing alone: their inability to remain at rest in a room.

Nothing.

The tape machine has stopped, the tape gone, The room stands still, although I sense movement just outside, or just inside, its walls. I stand up and look around. Three chairs, the colour of cheap ice-cream. And another phone, black, this one, its receiver in place but its plug removed from the wall socket. Another lies trussed on the floor, kidnapped. I move towards the closed door and as I open it, on the other side, a few feet further on, an open door begins to close. I push against the brown vinyl and this door opens, as the one behind me closes, as though they are separate yet attached in some invisible way.

•••

What is it that these spaces share, these spaces we have been asked to consider? We are told that it is power, but their real power lay elsewhere, in homes, in streets, inside, out there. No, what these spaces share is that they share space. Some of the spaces are dark, indeed, as are some of the spaces in which we view them, but let us consider a different form of dark space. In his study *Les Temps vécu* (1927), Eugène Minkowski presents 'a phenomenology of time and other fundamental categories of life together with a psychopathology of these categories as they are experienced by psychopathic persons'. One of these operative categories is, of course, space, and it is the final chapter, 'Towards a Psychopathology of Lived Space', which interests us here. Here, Minkowski uses the terms 'light space' and 'dark space' to distinguish between two different forms of lived space. These terms do not indicate

the physical characteristics of the space, however, although relative clarity and obscurity may contribute to the sense that Minkowski means, while extending far beyond these two descriptions.

In light space, I see objects with precise contours, objects beside each other, objects in relation to each other. I see the empty space between the objects also, but it seems less tangible than the objects themselves, and becomes their backdrop, dominated by their undeniable materiality. There may be sounds, also, although these sounds too are attached to objects I can see before me in space. And I am in this space also, at least one aspect of me is. I occupy the space exactly as the objects around me do, this space which becomes a 'public domain', a space which we share. But I do not give myself up to this space in totality; I keep a little of myself to myself, a part which repudiates this space. As such, I am able to give meaning to introspection, a 'looking inside' which only has meaning in relation to this light space, although what I may discover will not really be inside me.

'Now imagine a dark night, so obscure that you can see nothing: or achieve this absolute obscurity by closing your eyes and, as much as possible, shutting out everything that we know and can represent of light space. This obscurity is not at all the simple absence of light, as we know it; it has something very positive about it. It seems much more material to me, much more "filled" than light space, which, as we have seen, fades away, so to speak, before the materiality of the objects which are in it. Precisely because of this it does not spread out before me but touches me directly, envelops me, embraces me, even penetrates me, completely, passes through me, so that one could almost say that while the ego is permeable by darkness it is not permeable by light. The ego does not affirm itself in relation to darkness but becomes confused with it, becomes one with it.'

We see this occurring again and again in these spaces. Sounds are heard where no actions create them. A lens zooms but we see no camera; a subterranean corridor is filled with the sound of the wind blowing above, or water fountains miles away. People dissolve into their surroundings, through their adoption of uniforms initially (perhaps the most basic form of architecture), then taken wholly within, absorbed within lifts or split invisible inside mirrors.

> 'Everything is light, precise, and clear in light space. In dark space everything is obscure and mysterious. One feels as if in the presence of the unknown, in its positive value, and the phenomenon of "mystery" seems the best and most immediate way to express this characteristic trait of lived obscurity.'

Even in Vegas, with all those lights, was there ever a space so dark?

•••

After a press conference to launch his latest casino, I asked Steve Wynn about water. He said, 'Water is at the heart of the juxtaposition between fantasy and reality on which Las Vegas exists.'

•••

The corridors are beautiful, cool, a little wet. The lights running down their centre turn the walls to steel, to gold, the sheen making the polished Italian marble by turn industrial and precious. (Of course, this place is both simultaneously.) My eyes are drawn into the depth of the corridors, as if this isn't deep enough, invited, or perhaps more teased, as each movement forward leads only to an impenetrable surface, like the mirrors which reflect back the spaces while projecting them forward, through solids, into another space. Everything inside becomes outside. The perspective itself begins to shift and fails to resolve. Looking again, the space receding from the left seems higher than that on the right; indeed they look different, both different, one from the other. I am caught in an unresolved parallax where difference approximates a combined vision. Perhaps we have not passed through the mirror, into another space, but are caught in that space between mirror and glass, a space which flaunts its three-dimensionality while deprived of depth. Perhaps this space is simply a mirror, the mirror just a photograph.

I hear water fountains hissing outside Caesar's Palace. Outside, above, a monument is inscribed: 'Inspired by a vision of lonely lands made fruitful'.

•••

I find amongst some notes: 'Architecture of Entrapment, figure becomes split and fractured – it is absorbed into the architecture, for a fleeting moment it is revealed, then concealed again.' It's difficult to tell whether this is a description or a proposition.

•••

I go back to my room and lie on the bed, moving the books I had brought with me. Minkowski's *Lived Time*, unopened in this place of non-time, of graveyard time; and a book about this place. It's easier to read, and has pictures, so I keep hold of it, flicking its pages. 'Henri Bergson called disorder an order we cannot see.' 'Glittering in the dark: perimeters dark in value, absorbent in texture to obscure the extent and character of the architectural enclosure.' 'Maze for crowds of anonymous individuals without explicit connections with each other.' I am moving through the spaces again, the images moving before me, my body motionless. I carry on moving through the book, through its own spaces which open up, coinciding, perhaps, with the spaces before me, or passing through one another. There are more images: a Piranesi *carceri* and there I am, the figure in the picture, small and unclear, climbing dark stairs, or listening to that voice or reading De Quincey or, before that, moving through the chambers again, each mirroring the other, unable to tell which is the reflection, or which isn't.

At the end of the book, the architect of that other space appears: 'It is alright to decorate construction but never construct decoration.' The space is full of dust, slightly aerated. There are groups.

REFERENCES

p 14 'A small picture': Edgar Allan Poe, *The Fall of the House of Usher* (1840)

'I still saw the room': Eugène Minkowski, *Les Temps vécu* (1927)

p 16 'Creeping along the sides': Thomas de Quincey, *Confessions of an English Opium Eater* (1821)

p 17 'Oh, how will he make his way': Charles Nodier, *Piranèse, contes psychologiques, à propos de la monomanie réflective* (1836)

'it appeared to me': Fyodor Dostoyevsky, *The Gambler* (1866)

'The gambler': Walter Benjamin, *Passagen-Werk* (1927–40)

p 22 'Have not its incessant vagabondages': Walter Benjamin, *Passagen-Werk*

p 26 'That's it exactly': Edward Bellamy, *The Old Folk's Party* (1876)

p 29 'The air is still there': Eugène Minkowski, *Les Temps vécu*

p 39 'Now imagine a dark night': Eugène Minkowski, *Les Temps vécu*

p 40 'Everything is light': Eugène Minkowski, *Les Temps vécu*

'Architecture of Entrapment': notes written by Jane and Louise Wilson on *Vegas* edit board, displayed in Turner Prize exhibition

p 43 'Henri Bergson called disorder': Robert Venturi, Denise Scott Brown, Steven Izenour, *Learning from Las Vegas* (1972)

'It is alright to decorate construction': Pugin, quoted in Robert Venturi, Denise Scott Brown, Steven Izenour, *Learning from Las Vegas*

normapaths
1995

stasi city
1997

gamma
1999

'awaiting oblivion'

claire doherty

'Placeless places, beckoning thresholds, closed, forbidden spaces that are nevertheless exposed to the winds, hallways fanned by doors that open rooms for unbearable encounters and create gulfs between them across which voices cannot carry and that even muffle cries: corridors leading to more corridors where the night resounds, beyond sleep, with the smothered voices of those who speak, with the cough of the sick, with the walls of the dying, with the suspended breath of those who ceaselessly cease living; a long and narrow room, like a tunnel, in which approach and distance – the approach of forgetting, the distance of the wait – draw near to one another and unendingly move apart.'[1]

In these words Michel Foucault summons the fragmentary fictions of French philosopher and novelist Maurice Blanchot. Blanchot's texts are unsettling and complex, noted for their unerring sense of foreboding. They encapsulate the precarious existence of the modern individual through spatial metaphor. On reflection, Foucault might just as well have been describing the work of Jane and Louise Wilson.

The mental and physical process of disorientation, the oscillation between subject and object and the implication of death, surge as vividly through the Wilsons' video installations, still photographs and sculptural objects as they do through Blanchot's evocative texts. Their works certainly seem located somewhere 'beyond sleep', between fiction and reality. They encourage viewer, physical context and represented space to 'draw near to one another and move apart'. Their subject is estrangement, unease – the Uncanny.

Commentators have most recently immersed themselves in the historical potency of the Wilsons' found environments, in particular the decommissioned buildings of the Stasi headquarters in Berlin (*Stasi City*, 1997) and US Air Force base at Greenham Common (*Gamma*, 1999). The artists themselves continue to investigate potential sites of dramatic narrative. Yet it would be to do Jane and Louise Wilson a disservice to suggest that their works operate merely to invoke the 'architectural uncanny' for the sake of theatre. A consideration of their work, mindful of Foucault's own theorisation of spatial conditions, reveals an ongoing fascination with the divergent architectural, psychic and social manifestations of power. Their filmic journeys and kaleidoscopic views are not just spectacular responses to site, but visually compelling investigations into the tension between control and resistance.

In her analysis of the structure of war, Elaine Scarry defines 'consent' as the primary value used to differentiate war from torture – the ethical loophole for moral distance in which the idea of resistance is denied. Whilst 'nuclear arms may at first appear a radical extension of freedom,' she argues, 'human presence is eliminated, so the human act of consent is eliminated ... Consent is in nuclear war a structured impossibility.'[2] The Wilsons' still photographs of the interior of the former cruise-missile base record the control panels, ventilation units and decontamination chambers, often using a single light source, from a low viewpoint, exaggerating the sheer functionality of the site. Such an interior belies the history of Greenham Common itself – one of reoccurring struggle over consent – a history defined through a series of trade-offs between district councils, government ministries and corporate business interests.[3] The base, like the former Stasi headquarters, Houses of Parliament and Caesar's Palace, embodies a form of social control. Such spaces are contained and containing, distinguished from the 'normal' spaces of the city, marked by the abnormal human behaviour which is sanctioned within their walls. Consent is the fulcrum of their existence, explicit or implicit.

In his theorisation of spatial conditions, Foucault identified a late-18th-century shift in Western cultural power from a coercive form of social control, meted out by the sovereign, to a more diffuse and insidious form of social surveillance and process of 'normalisation'. The latter, Foucault claims, was encapsulated by Jeremy Bentham's Panopticon, a 19th-century prison system in which prison cells were arranged around a central watchtower.

'These cells have two windows, one opening on to the inside, facing the windows of the central tower, the other, outer one allowing daylight to pass through the whole cell. All that is then needed is to put an overseer in the tower and place in each of the cells a lunatic, a patient, a convict, or a schoolboy. The back lighting enables one to pick out from the central tower the little captive silhouettes in the ring of cells. In short, the principle of the dungeon is reversed; daylight and the overseer's gaze capture the inmate more effectively than darkness, which afforded after all a sort of protection.'[4]

The Panopticon is thus a metaphor for the process whereby disciplinary architecture (and technologies) police both the mind and body of the modern individual. 'There is no need for arms, physical violence, material constraints,' Foucault asserts. 'Just a gaze. An inspecting gaze, a gaze which each individual under its weight will end by interiorisation to the point that he is his own overseer, each individual thus exercising this surveillance over, and against, himself. A superb formula: of power exercised continuously and for what turns out to be minimal cost.'[5]

It is this transparency of surveillance imposed under the auspices of protection and care which interests the Wilsons.[6] From the implied complicity of *Hypnotic Suggestion 505* (1993) to the beguiling kitsch of *Las Vegas, Graveyard Time* (1999), their work reveals the mechanism of coercion under the absent yet omnipresent 'eye of power'. The obvious distinction between their earlier work and more recent investigations is a shift away from the human figure (usually one or both of the artists) as sole metaphor for the complicit subject to depopulated sites, which resonate with implied social control.

Empty but for the deliberate insertion of props, these loaded sites of historical significance are stripped of anecdote and consequently each begins to resemble the scene of a crime. When the figures of the artists do appear, it is in costume, acting out the role of a demonstration model, rather than as characters in their own right. The sites are filmed and photographed, and in some cases reconstructed, as if for the establishment of evidence. The gnawing absence in *Parliament, A Third House*, *Stasi City*, *Gamma* and *Las Vegas, Graveyard Time* seems to signify some kind of traumatic occurrence. Yet only the bare architectural and technological structures remain. Certainly the works use the filmic devices of the thriller to build suspense. The vocabulary of disorientation is employed – labyrinthine space, reoccurring features, mirroring, undisclosed exits and anonymous subjects – to full effect. Yet, if the conceit of narrative is absent, what are these devices used to signify?

The Wilsons' development from the single-screen projection (and singular viewpoint) in *Crawl Space* (1995) to their most recent multi-screen installations has resulted in the overt implication of the viewer in the work. The artists play upon our preconceptions, at once denying and implicating the histories that have been projected onto the various sites. Their investigative process recalls the unfulfilled tourist quest for authenticity. To 'the outside', such places are mediated abstracts, dislocated from lived experience, their referent activities – government, gambling, intelligence, nuclear war – more dramatic than their architectural prosthetics.

Whilst previously the deserted nature of the redundant sites of *Stasi City* and *Gamma* was contingent, the emptiness of *Parliament, A Third House* and *Las Vegas, Graveyard Time* (customarily mediated to us through vociferous activity) confirms the Wilsons' insistence on the viewer as sole occupant of the space. Further, it is through their considered use of distortion and doubling that a prescribed meaning or history for each site is eschewed.

The uncanny or *unheimlich*, according to Freud's definition of 1919, is invoked through the recognition that something is missing, something familiar has suddenly become defamiliarised, as if in a dream. This nightmarish quality is heightened in the Wilsons' work through the propensity of the double. For example, in *Reconstruction of Doors, Erich Mielke's Office, Former Stasi Headquarters* (1997), installed at Kunstverein, Graz in 1998 with stills of the Höhenschonhausen prison, the Wilsons perform a literal doubling of the mimetic process. The three-dimensional doorways and double doors jutting into the space appear at once representations of the photograph and of the site. The viewer is positioned at a point of multiple entries and exits. The confusion engendered by the multiplicity of partial views replicates the prisoner's psychological condition.

This doubling occurs once again in the recent photographs of Caesar's Palace – the exits obscured by a seemingly endless array of fruit machines and mirrored ceilings which lead the player ever downwards back towards the card tables and 'high rollers'.

It is an effect which recalls the dream sequences of film director Stanley Donen, whereby the central characters (Gene Kelly, Audrey Hepburn, Fred Astaire) on reaching an impasse, are transported from the 'reality' of the film's narrative to a theatrical labyrinth. The 'ballet' is performed through a series of encounters with contradictory spaces – entrances as exits, inner walls that cloak interiors and so on – until exhaustion (loss of self) or resolution.

Architectural historian Anthony Vidler has described such an effect in relation to the architectural uncanny, comparing it to the condition of schizophrenia. Here he suggests, in reponse to the question, 'where are you?', the schizophrenic response would be, 'I know where I am, but I do not feel as though I'm at the spot where I find myself.'[7] The absence of 'anchors' in the Wilsons' work (whether human figures or legible exit points) thus induces a condition similar to that of schizophrenia or spatial phobia.

Even within Pugin's supremely uplifting Houses of Parliament, the Wilsons weave a network of conflicting sightlines using mirrors and stereoscopic filming. The resulting kaleidoscopic video installation reflects the artifice of government, creating a highly pertinent metaphor for a 'spun' constitution. Even here, within the primary locus of democracy, the environment is defamiliarised so that the viewer's status as official 'stranger' (with consent but without freedom) is signified. The humming presence of the pipe vaults act as a metaphor for the hidden apparatus of government. The Wilsons' films have the capacity to instil fear, not only because they use the mechanism of suspense, but precisely because they dislocate us from the superficial, indicating the systems of our own subjugation.

In *Awaiting Oblivion*, a piece dedicated to Samuel Beckett, Maurice Blanchot wrote of resistance as 'that voice or rumble or murmur which is always under the threat of silence, that undifferentiated speech, affirming beneath all affirmation, impossible to negate, too weak to be silenced, too docile to be constrained ... living among the dead, dead among the living.'[8] His words recall the women of Greenham Common, whose keening protest along the perimeter disturbed the regulatory composure of the military base. The associated sound of spoons dragging across a fence is heard as a faint and incessant soundtrack to *Gamma* – a warning – 'living among the dead, dead among the living'. In its economy, this disruption indicates the Wilsons' adept response to location, in which they resist a didactic narrative in favour of the transparent contradictions of their chosen subject. Here against the possibility of oblivion, the sound of repressed consent, is deafening.

1 Michel Foucault, 'Maurice Blanchot: The Thought from Outside', in *Foucault/Blanchot*, translated by Jeffrey Mehiman and Brian Massumi, New York, Zone Books, 1987, p xxxix

2 Elaine Scarry, *The Body in Pain*, Oxford University Press, 1985, p 152

3 See Gilda Williams, 'Jane and Louise Wilson', *Art Monthly*, issue 225, April 1999, pp 26–27

4 Michel Foucault, *Power/Knowledge: Selected Interviews and Other Writings 1972–1977*, edited by Colin Gordon, Pantheon Books, New York, 1980, p 153

5 *op.cit.*

6 See 'In Stereoscopic Vision: A dialogue between Jane and Louise Wilson and Lisa Corrin', *Jane and Louise Wilson*, Serpentine Gallery, 1999, pp 8–12

7 Anthony Vidler, *The Architectural Uncanny: Essays in the Modern Unhomely*, MIT, Massachusetts, 1992, p 174

8 Maurice Blanchot, *Awaiting Oblivion*, translated by John Gregg, University of Nebraska Press, p 36

lists

JANE AND LOUISE WILSON

1986–89   Duncan of Jordanstone College of Art, Dundee, BA Fine Art (Louise);
          Newcastle Polytechnic, BA Fine Art (Jane)
1990–92   Goldsmiths' College, London, MA Fine Art (Jane and Louise)
1993   Barclays Young Artist Award
1996   DAAD Scholarship, Berlin/Hannover
1999   Nominated for the Turner Prize
2000   IASPIS (International Artists Studio Program in Sweden), Stockholm,
          Residency, autumn 2000

TWO-PERSON EXHIBITIONS

2000   *Star City*, 303 Gallery, New York
           Bernier/Eliades, Athens
           Stasi City & Crawl Space, MIT List Visual Arts Centre, Cambridge,
           Massachusetts
1999/2000 *Turner Prize*, Tate Gallery, London
1999   *Gamma*, Lisson Gallery, London
           Stasi City, Hamburger Kunsthalle, Hamburg
           Jane and Louise Wilson, Serpentine Gallery, London
1998   *H&R Projects*, Brussels
           Stasi City, 303 Gallery, New York
           Film Stills, Aki-Ex Gallery, Tokyo
1997   *Stasi City*, Kunstverein Hannover (touring to Kunstraum Munich; Centre
           d'art Contemporain, Geneva; Kunstwerke, Berlin)
           Jane and Louise Wilson, London Electronic Arts, London
1996   Galleria S.A.L.E.S., Rome (part of the British Art Festival)
1995   *Normapaths*, Chisenhale Gallery, London (touring to Berwick Gymnasium
           Gallery, Berwick-upon-Tweed)
           Crawl Space, Milch Gallery, London
1994   *Crawl Space*, British Project II, Galerie Krinzinger, Vienna
           Routes 1 & 9 North, AC Project Room, New York

GROUP EXHIBITIONS

2000   Historisches Museum, Frankfurt
           'Conversione di Saulo', Palazzo Odescalchi, Rome
           'Vision and Reality', Louisiana Museum of Modern Art, Copenhagen
           'Media_City Seoul 2000', Seoul
           'Annika von Hausswolf, Jane & Louise Wilson and Weegee', Magasin 3,
           Konsthall, Stockholm
           'A Shot in the Head', Lisson Gallery, London
           'Film/Video Works – Lisson Gallery at 9 Keane Street', Lisson Gallery
           MIT List Visual Arts Center, Cambridge

'Images Festival', Toronto

'Dream Machines', curated by Susan Hiller, Dundee Contemporary Arts, Scotland, touring to Mappin Art Gallery, Sheffield and Camden Arts Centre, London

'Age of influence: reflections in the mirror of American culture', Museum of Contemporary Art, Chicago

'Point of View – Works from a Private Collection', Richard Salmon Gallery, London

'Art, Science & Technology', New Greenham Enterprise, Newbury

1999 'Trace', Liverpool Biennial, Tate Liverpool

'This Other World of Ours', TV Gallery, Moscow

Chac Mool Contemporary Fine Art, West Hollywood, in collaboration with Lisson Gallery

'Clues', Monte Video – Netherlands Media Art Institute, Amsterdam

'Carnegie International: CI:99', Carnegie Museum, Pittsburgh

'Seeing Time: Selections from the Pamela and Richard Kramlich Collection of Media Art', San Francisco Museum of Modern Art

1998 'View 1', Mary Boone, New York

'In the meantime', Galeria Estrany de la Mota, Barcelona

'Spectacular Optical', Threadwaxing Space, New York

'Earth, Water, Air', D C Moore, New York

'Then and Now', Lisson Gallery, London

'Mise en Scène', Grazer Kunstverein, Graz

'Black Box', touring exhibition, Film and Video Umbrella, London

'Malos Habitos', Soledad Lorenzo Gallery, Madrid

1997 'Hyperamnesiac Fabulations', The Power Plant, Toronto

'Remake – Re-model', Centrum Beeldende Kunst, Rotterdam

'Ein Stuck Vom Himmel', Kunsthalle Nuremburg

'Follow Me – Britische Kunst an der Unterelbe', billboards between Buxtehude and Cuxhaven

'Picturea Britannica', Museum of Contemporary Art, Sydney (touring to Art Gallery South Australia, Adelaide; City Gallery, Wellington)

'Broken Home', Greene Naftali, New York

'Hospital', Galerie Max Hetzler, Berlin

'Instant', Green Room, Manchester

1996 'Co-operators', Southampton City Art Gallery (touring to Huddersfield Art Gallery)

'Ace! Arts Council New Purchases', Hatton Gallery, Newcastle (touring to Harris Museum, Preston; Ikon Gallery, Birmingham; Mappin Art Gallery, Sheffield; Angel Row, Nottingham; Ormeau Baths, Belfast; Hayward Gallery, London)

'NowHere', Louisiana Museum, Humlebaek

'Auto reverse 2', Le Magasin, Grenoble
'Young British Artists', Roslyn Oxley Gallery, Paddington (Australia)
'More Than Real', Palazzo Reale, Caserta
'Trailer', Ynglingagatan Gallery, Stockholm
'Der Umbau Raum', Kunstlerhaus Stuttgart
'British Artists', Rhona Hoffman Gallery, Chicago
'Nach Weimar', Kunstsammlungen zu Weimar
'Quatros Duplos', Fundaçao Calouste Gulbenkian, Lisbon
'Files', Bunker, Berlin
'Full House', Kunstmuseum Wolfsburg
'Attitude Adjustment', 5th New York Video Festival, Lincoln Center, New York
'Dei Popoli', Filmfestival, Florence

1995   'The British Art Show 4', South Bank Centre exhibition, touring to Edinburgh, Manchester, Cardiff
'Young British Artists', Eigen + Art, Independent Art Space, London
'Corpus Delicti: London in the 1990s', Kunstforeningen, Copenhagen
'Kine Kunst '95', Casino Knokke
'Speaking of Sofas …', Soho House, London
'Mysterium Alltag', Kampnagel, Hamburg (with Jane Wilson, Gillian Wearing, Tracey Emin, Tacita Dean)
'General Release', British Council selection for Venice Biennale, Scuola San Pasquale, Venice
'Here and Now', Serpentine Gallery, London
'Fuori Uso', Stabilimenti Ex-Aurum, Pescara
'Wild Walls', Stedelijk Museum, Amsterdam
'Inferno 1', Galleria Raucci/Santamaria, Naples
'Gang Warfare', Independent Art Space, London
'Kunst aus London, Mysterium Alltag', Hammoniales Festival der Frauen, Hamburg
'Instant', Camden Arts Centre, London

1994   'Beyond Belief', Lisson Gallery, London
'Domestic Violence', Gio Marconi, Milan
'Facts of Life', Galerie 102, Dusseldorf
'Audience 0.01', Trevi Art Museum, Trevi
'New Reality Mix', 18 Hogbergsgatan, Stockholm
'The Ecstasy of Limits', Gallery 400, University of Illinois, Chicago
Galerie Valeria Belvedere, Milan
'Use Your Allusion. Recent Video Art', Museum of Contemporary Art, Chicago
'Le Shuttle', Kunstlerhaus Bethanien, Berlin

1993–94 'BT New Contemporaries', Cornerhouse, Manchester (touring to Orchard

Gallery, Derry, Mappin Art Gallery, Sheffield, City Museum and Art Gallery, Stoke-on-Trent, Centre for Contemporary Arts, Glasgow)

1993   'Barclays Young Artists', Serpentine Gallery, London
      'Underlay', Renwick Street, New York
      'The Daily Planet', Transmission Gallery, Glasgow
      'Over the Limit', Arnolfini, Bristol
      'Summer Show', David Zwirner Gallery, New York
      'Wonderful Life', Lisson Gallery, London
      'Lucky Kunst', Silver Place, London
      'Close Up', 42nd Street, New York
      'Walter Benjamin's Briefcase', Moagens, Oporto

1992   'Inside a Microcosm, Summer Show', Laure Genillard Gallery, London
      'Into the Nineties 4', Mall Galleries, London

SELECT BIBLIOGRAPHY

2000   *Artecinema*, Teatro Sannazaro, Naples
      Media_City Seoul 2000, Seoul
      Annika von Hausswolf, Jane & Louise Wilson and Weegee, Konsthall, Stockholm
      Conversione di Saulo, Palazzo Odescalchi, Rome

1999   *Jane & Louise Wilson*, Serpentine Gallery, London
      Carnegie International: CI:99, Carnegie Museum, Pittsburgh

1998   *Black Box*, Film and Video Umbrella, London

1997   *Stasi City*, Hannover Kunstverein, Hannover

1996   *Co-operators*, Southampton City Art Gallery, Southampton
      NowHere, Louisiana Museum, Humlebaek
      Artisti Britannici a Roma, Umberto Allemandi, Turin

1995   *Normapaths*, Chisenhale Gallery, London
      Here and Now, Serpentine Gallery, London
      General Release, British Council, Venice
      The British Art Show 4, Cornerhouse, Manchester

1993   *BT New Contemporaries*, Cornerhouse, Manchester
      Over the Limit, Arnolfini, Bristol

INDEX OF PICTURES